CW01280733

**Learning Tree
1 2 3**

What's Next?

By Richard and Nicky Hales
Illustrated by Rebecca Mason

CHERRYTREE BOOKS

As you read this book, try to answer the questions, and try to think of some questions of your own.
Write your answers on a piece of paper or in a notebook – not in the book.
There are answers at the end of the book. Try not to look at them before you have had a try. If you find the questions difficult, ask a grown-up or older friend to help you.

A Cherrytree Book

Designed and produced by
A S Publishing

First published 1990
by Cherrytree Press Ltd
a subsidiary of
The Chivers Company Ltd
Windsor Bridge Road
Bath, Avon BA2 3AX

Copyright © Cherrytree Press Ltd 1990

British Library Cataloguing in Publication Data
Hales, Richard
 What's next?
 1. Mathematics
 I. Title II. Hales, Nicky III. Mason, Rebecca IV. Series
 510

ISBN 0-7451-5090-X

Printed and bound in Italy by L.E.G.O. s.p.a., Vicenza

All rights reserved. No part of this publication may be reproduced, stored in a retrieval system, or transmitted, in any form or by any means without the prior permission in writing of the publisher, nor be otherwise circulated in any form of binding or cover other than that in which it is published and without a similar condition including this condition being imposed on the subsequent purchaser.

What's next?

red lorry   yellow lorry   red lorry

Can you say this quickly over and over again?

What do you think will happen next?

What do you think will happen next?

What do you think will happen next?

Draw what comes next on a piece of paper.

7

Monday   Tuesday   Wednesday

What day comes next?

8

Draw what you think will be in the last picture.

spring

summer

autumn

Draw your answers on a piece of paper.

Which way next?

Where next?

Where will the next face be?

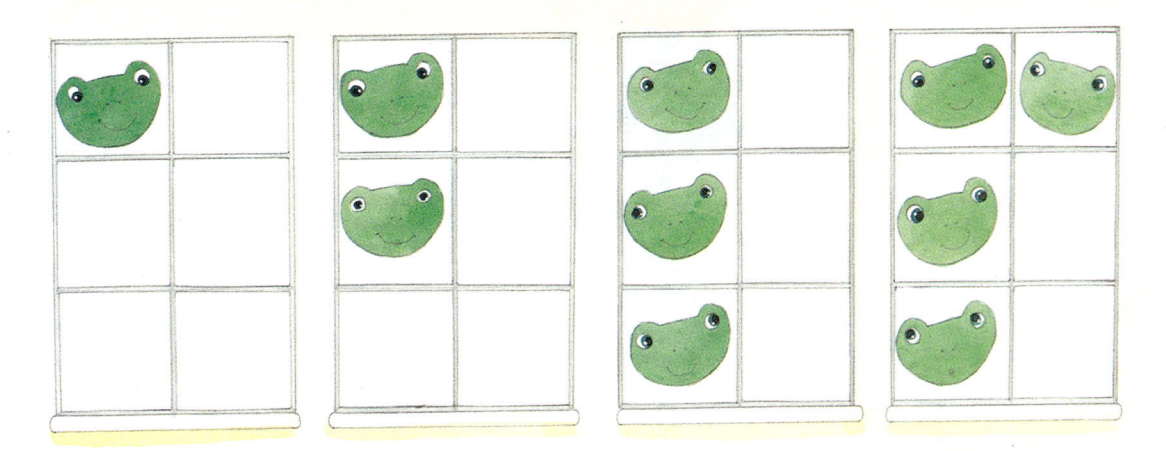

Which quarter of pizza will the last frog eat?

How old is the last frog?

How many frogs should be in the last boat?

12

What number comes next?

1 3 5 7 →

10 9 8 7 →

12 13 14 15 →

2 4 6 8 →

What letter comes next?

DEFDEF →

AbCdEfGhI →

BDF →

What comes next?

A set of things in order is called a sequence.
Can you follow these sequences?
Do you know what comes next?

a a b c c d e e f g →

A B C E F G I J K →

Z Y X W V U T S →

A to Z

Can you carry on to the end of the alphabet?

first　　second　　third　　fourth　　?

short　　shorter　　shortest

long　　longer　　?

16

What time is it?

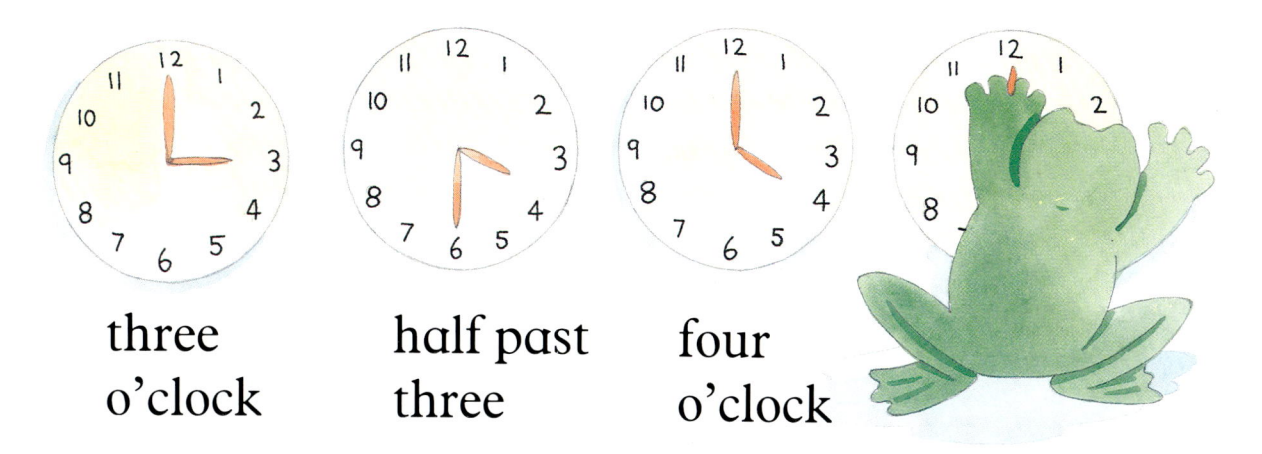

three o'clock   half past three   four o'clock

What month comes next?

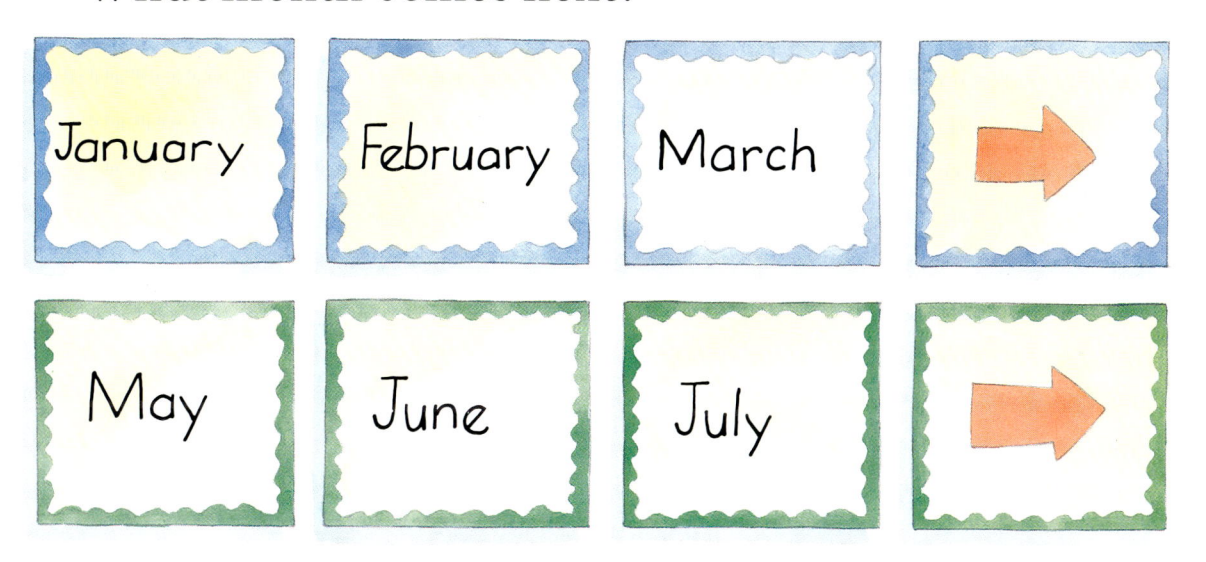

| January | February | March | ➡ |
| May | June | July | ➡ |

Can you go on to the end of the year?

17

5, 10 15 20 →

10 20 30 40 →

Can you go all the way to 100?

What number does the blue frog live at?

What number does the green frog live at?

4 7 10 13

Too hard for me!

Whatever next?

Tell the story in the right order.

20

That's easy!

What more?

Using this book
Keep a maths notebook and put the answers to the questions in it. Think of your own questions and put those in too.

Do not write or draw in this book. Someone else may want to use it after you.

Try to answer the questions before you look at the answers. If your answer is different from the one in the book, try again.

Always check your answers. If your answer is different from the one in the book, it may still be right. Sometimes there is more than one answer.

Think about order
Think about what comes next. Which do you have first, your pudding or your main course? How do you dress in the morning? Do you put your coat on before your vest? Your shoes before your socks?

What do you do first when you get up in the morning? What else do you do before you go to school? Make sure you put all these in the right order.
What does the sun do in the morning? What does it do at mid-day? What does it do in the evening?

Make a pattern
Get some coloured bricks or buttons. Line them up in a sequence, like this: red, blue, yellow, green, red, blue, yellow, green and so on, or blue, red, red, yellow, blue, red, red, yellow.

Toys in order
Line up some of your toys beginning with the smallest and ending with the largest.

Family in order
Draw your family, starting with the youngest and ending with the oldest.

Traffic lights
Watch the traffic lights. Try to learn the sequence of colours. The orange colour is called amber.

1

1 Draw four pictures in the right order to show what you do before school in the morning.

2 Draw these in order, starting with the slowest and ending with the fastest – bicycle, rocket, aeroplane, car.

3 Draw these in order, starting with the fastest and ending with the slowest – rabbit, leopard, horse, tortoise.

4 What number comes next? Three, four, five,

5 What will happen next?

2

6 Draw an apple. Take a bite from it and draw the apple again. Take another bite and make another drawing. Carry on until only the core is left.

7 What comes before summer and after winter?

8 What day comes after Saturday?

9 What number comes next? Five, four, three

10 The gold medallist comes first. The silver medallist comes second. Where does the bronze medallist come?

11 Put these animals in order of size, starting with the smallest – horse, ant, rabbit, dog, rhinoceros.

12 Line your family up in order of size. Who is tallest? Who is smallest?

3

13 What number is your house? What number is the house next door?

14 This rhyme is out of order. Can you move one line to put it in the right order?
  Jack and Jill went up the hill
  And Jill came tumbling after.
  To fetch a pail of water.
  Jack fell down and broke his crown

15 Find out what time school starts. When lunch begins and ends. What time school finishes.

16 What number comes next?
1 5 9 13

17 What letter comes next?
F E D C

18 The words in this sentence are jumbled up. Can you put them in the right order?
Cat mat the on sat.

19 What is your favourite television programme? Find out the name of the programme before it and the name of the programme after it.

Answers to 123
2 bicycle
car
aeroplane
rocket
3 tortoise
rabbit
horse
leopard
4 six
5 The frogs will shake hands
7 spring
8 Sunday
9 two
10 third
11 ant
rabbit
dog
horse
rhinoceros
14 Move the second line to the end.
16 17
17 B
18 The cat sat on the mat

23

Index

1 2 3 22, 23
100 18
1st 2nd 3rd 16
alphabet 15
answers 21, 23, 24
ask questions 21
boats 12
check your answers 21
day and night 8
days 8
faces at the window 10, 11
family in order 21
first, second, third 16
fish 3
how many frogs? 12
how old? 12

long, longer 16
make a pattern 21
Monday, Tuesday, Wednesday 8
months 17
notebook 21
pizza 11
red lorry, yellow lorry 3
road closed 4
sequence 15
short, shorter, shortest 16
spring, summer, autumn 9
tell the story 20
think about order 21
toys in order 21

traffic lights 21
questions 21, 22, 23
using this book 21
what day? 8
whatever next? 19
what letter? 14, 15
what month? 17
what more? 21
what number? 13, 18, 19
what's next? 3, 6, 7
what time? 17
what will happen 3, 5
where next? 10
which way? 10
year 17

Answers

Page 8
night
Thursday

Page 9
winter

Page 10
[grid with dot]

Page 11
[grid with dots]

Page 12
6 years old
2 frogs

Page 13
9
6
16
10

Page 14
D
j
H

Page 15
g
M
R

Page 16
fifth
longest

Page 17
half past four
April
August

Page 18
25
50

Page 19
24
25
16